JAMESTOWN

Heritage

READERS

Book A

Lee Mountain, Ed.D.
University of Houston, Texas

Sharon Crawley, Ed.D.
Florida Atlantic University

Edward Fry, Ph.D.
Professor Emeritus
Rutgers University

Jamestown Publishers
Providence, Rhode Island

Favorite Children's Classics

ILLUSTRATED BY THE BEST ARTISTS
FROM THE PAST AND PRESENT

Jamestown Heritage Readers, Book A
Catalog No. 951
Catalog No. 951H, Hardcover Edition

© 1991 by Jamestown Publishers, Inc.

Cover and text design by Deborah Hulsey Christie
Cover and border illustrations by Pamela R. Levy

Printed in the United States of America

3   4   5   6   7   HA   97   96   95   94   93

ISBN 0-89061-951-4
ISBN 0-89061-710-4, Hardcover Edition

C·O·N·T·E·N·T·S

ONE
Tales Retold

T W O

Here and There, Then and Now

THREE
The Whole Story

FOUR
Numbers, Nature, and Nonsense

UNIT ONE

Tales
Retold

Little Boy Blue

from

MOTHER GOOSE

Little Boy Blue
Come blow your horn.
The sheep's in the meadow.
The cow's in the corn.

But where is the boy
Who looks after the sheep?
He's under the hay stack,
Fast asleep.

Jack and Jill

from
MOTHER GOOSE

Jack and Jill
Went up the hill
To fetch a pail of water.
Jack fell down
And broke his crown,
And Jill came tumbling after.

9

Mary Had a Little Lamb

from

MOTHER GOOSE

Mary had a little lamb.

Its fleece was white as snow.

And everywhere that Mary went

The lamb was sure to go.

Why does the lamb love Mary so?

The other children cry.

Why, Mary loves the lamb, you know,

Her mother did reply.

Old Mother Hubbard

from

MOTHER GOOSE

Old Mother Hubbard
Went to the cupboard
To get her poor dog a bone.

When she got there
The cupboard was bare,
So the poor dog had none.

Little Red Riding Hood

by

CHARLES PERRAULT

There was once a little girl.
She lived near the woods.

Her mother loved her very much.
Her grandma loved her even more.
So her grandma made a red hood
for her. She wore it all the time.

That is why her friends
called her Little Red Riding Hood.

One day her mother baked
some cakes.

"Your grandma likes my baking,"
she said to Little Red Riding Hood.
"Please take these cakes to her."

On her way through the woods
the little girl met a wolf.

He was a very hungry wolf.
He wanted to eat her up right away.
But he could not, because there were
wood cutters nearby.

"Good day, little girl," he said.
"Where are you going?"

"I am going to see my grandma,"
she said. "I have some cakes for her."

"I see," said the hungry wolf.
"Does your grandma live far from here?"

"No," said Little Red Riding Hood.
"She lives on the other side of the woods."

"I will go see her, too," said the wolf.
"You take this road. And I will take
the other road. We will see who gets
there first."

15

The wolf took the shorter way.

Soon he was at Grandma's house.

The wolf knocked at her door.

"Who is there?" called Grandma.

"Little Red Riding Hood," he said.
The hungry wolf made his voice
sound like a little girl's voice.
"I have brought you some cakes."

"Come in," said Grandma.

The hungry wolf opened the door.
He jumped at her to eat her up.

But she was too quick for him.
She ran into the side room and hid.

Then he heard Red Riding Hood
coming. The hungry wolf hopped
into the bed. He pulled the blankets
up to his neck.

17

"Hello, Grandma," said Little
Red Riding Hood as she walked in.

"Come over by me," said the wolf.
He tried to sound like her grandma.

She walked over to the bed.
Red Riding Hood was surprised to see
how strange her grandma looked.

"What big ears you have," she said.

"The better to hear you with,
my dear," said the wolf.

"What big eyes you have," she said.

"The better to see you with, my dear,"
said the wolf.

"What big hands you have," she said.

"The better to grab you with,
my dear," said the wolf.

"What big teeth you have," she said.

"The better to eat you up, my dear!"
And the wolf jumped at her!

Just then a wood cutter came in.
With one blow he cut off the wolf's head.

Grandma and Red Riding Hood
thanked the wood cutter for saving them.

Then the three of them sat down
and ate the cakes together.

There Was a Little Girl

by

HENRY WADSWORTH LONGFELLOW

There was a little girl

Who had a little curl

Right in the middle of her forehead.

When she was good

She was very, very good.

But when she was bad, she was horrid.

The Golden Goose

by the

BROTHERS GRIMM

Once there was a man who had
three sons. The older two were selfish.
But the youngest son was not selfish.
His name was Dumkin.

One day the oldest son went out
to cut wood. His mother gave him
a nice sweet cake to take with him.

In the woods he met a little old man.

"Please give me some cake," said the man.

The oldest son said, "No. It is all mine."

Then he went to cut down a tree.

But he hurt his arm and had to go home.

23

The second son now had to go
to the forest to cut wood.

His mother gave him a sweet cake
to take with him.

In the woods he met the same
little old man.

"Please give me some cake,"
said the little old man. "I am
so hungry."

The second son said, "No.
If I give you some of my cake,
I won't have enough for myself.
Get out of my way!"

The second son walked away
from the hungry old man. But soon
he hurt his leg and had to go home.

Then Dumkin, the youngest son,
went to cut wood in the forest.

His mother had no more cakes.
So she gave him only bread.

In the woods he met the same man.
"Give me some cake, please," he said.

"I have only bread," said Dumkin.
"But we can eat it together."

When Dumkin pulled out his bread,
it had turned by magic into cake.

Then the little old man said,
"You gave me some of your food.
Now I will give you something."

He walked over to an old tree.
"In this trunk is something for you,"
he said. Then he walked away.

Dumkin cut down the tree.

When it fell, he saw a goose sitting on the trunk. Its feathers were of gold!

He took it with him to a farmhouse. Dumkin stayed there that night.

The farmer had three daughters. When they saw Dumkin's goose, they wanted its golden feathers.

The oldest girl hid in his room. She thought, "When he is asleep, I can pull out a feather."

But when she touched the goose,
her hand stuck to it.

Soon the second sister came in.
She, too, wanted a gold feather.
But when she touched her sister,
she found herself stuck.

Then came the third sister.
The other two cried, "Keep away!"

As soon as she touched them,
she too was stuck. So they all
had to pass the night like this.

The next day Dumkin left
with his goose. He did nothing
about the girls running behind him.

In the field they met their father.
"Why do you run after that boy?"
he cried. "Stop! Come home."

He took hold of his youngest girl.
He tried to pull her away. No sooner
had he touched her than he was stuck.
He, too, had to run behind.

When the cook saw the farmer,
he cried, "Where are you going?"
He pulled the farmer by the arm.
But then he could not get away.

The cook cried, "Help!"

Two farm workers ran to him,
and got stuck.

Soon they reached a town.
In this town lived a king who had
a daughter. She never laughed.

The king had said, "The man
who makes my daughter laugh
can marry her."

When she saw seven people running
one after another, she started laughing.
She laughed as if she would never stop.
So Dumkin was given the princess's hand.

And that is how it happened that
Dumkin became a prince.
He was kind and nice.
So good things
came his way.

The Princess and the Pea

by

HANS CHRISTIAN ANDERSEN

Once upon a time there was a Prince.

He wanted to marry a princess. But she had to be a real princess. She had to be fine in every way.

He met many girls who said they were princesses.

But there was always something not quite right about each girl. Not one seemed fine in every way.

34

The Prince was sad. He wished
so much to have a real princess
for his wife.

His mother wanted to help him.
So she thought of a test for a princess.
But she would not tell even the Prince
how it would work.

"We will use my test soon," she said.
"We will use it on the next girl who
comes here and says she is a princess."

35

One night heavy rain started
to fall. The Prince heard a knock
at the door. His father, the King, went
to open it.

The girl standing there was wet
through and through.

"I am a princess from another land,"
she said. "I am looking for the Prince
who wants to meet a real princess."

"Come in," said the King.

The Prince looked for her horse.
But she had no horse. Wouldn't
a real princess have a horse?

He looked at her clothes.
She was not dressed like a princess.

But somehow she still seemed
fine in every way.

"If only I could be sure she is
a real princess," he thought.

His mother said to the girl,
"You must stay here tonight.
We will fix a bed for you."

"I hope she is a real princess,"
the Prince told his mother.

"I will give her my test,"
she said. "Then we will know."

The Prince's mother would not tell
him what she was going to do.

But she went into the bedroom
where the princess would sleep.
And she took one little pea with her.

It was hard, like a tiny stone.
She put the pea on the bed.

Then she put a soft mattress on top
of the pea. And then another mattress.
And another!

Soon she had piled ten mattresses on top of the pea. And then ten more!

The bed was so high that the girl had to climb a ladder to get on it.

"Good night," said the Queen.

"Good night," said the princess.

"I wonder how the bed will feel to her," thought the Queen. "Is she so fine that she can feel a pea through all those mattresses? We shall see."

The next morning the Queen was
up early. So was the princess.

"How did you sleep?" asked the Queen.

"Not well at all," said the princess.
"You were kind to let me stay here.
So I'm sorry to say I couldn't sleep.
There was something hard in my bed.
I am black and blue from rolling on it."

The Queen called for her son.

"We have found a princess
who can pass my test," she said.
"Only a real true princess could feel
a pea through so many mattresses."

So the Prince and the real princess
were married. And they lived happily
ever after.

The Boy Who Cried Wolf

from
AESOP'S FABLES

Once there was a boy who took care of sheep.

He was told to call, "Wolf," if he saw a wolf coming. Then people would run to help him.

One day he thought of a trick he could play.

"If I cry 'Wolf,' people will run up here to me," he said to himself. "That would be fun."

So he cried, "The wolf is here!
Help me!"

Men and women came running.

But when they reached him,
they saw at once that the wolf
was not there.

A man shook his head at the boy.
"You were just fooling us," he said.
"You were not telling the truth."

All the people went away.

The next day the boy thought
it would be fun to fool the people
a second time.

He cried, "Wolf! Help me!"
Again people ran to help him.
Again they saw that
the wolf was not there.

"No more
of your lies!"
said a woman.

Then one day the wolf really
did come.

The boy cried, "Wolf! Wolf!"
But this time the people did not come.

So the boy ran down the hill,
calling for help.

The first man he met said,
"You cried wolf before.
But the wolf had not come."
The next man said,
"You are not telling the truth.
You want to fool us again."
No one helped him.
So the wolf had time to kill
a sheep and eat it, since no one
believed the boy who cried wolf.

**Liars are not believed
even when they tell the truth.**

Block City

by

ROBERT LOUIS STEVENSON

What are you able
To build with your blocks?
Castles and palaces,
Houses and docks.

Rain may keep raining
And others may roam.
But I can be happy
While building at home.

Rain, Rain, Go Away
ANONYMOUS

Rain, rain, go away.
Come again another day.
Little Johnny wants to play.

49

Tug of War
from an
AFRICAN LEGEND

Rabbit lived on the same island
with Elephant and Hippo.

Elephant lived on one side.

Hippo lived on the other side.

Rabbit lived in the middle.

Elephant and Hippo laughed
at Rabbit because he was not strong.
So he thought of a trick to play on them.

He took a heavy rope with him.
And he went to see Elephant.

"Good day, Elephant," he said.
"Which of us do you think is stronger?"

"What a silly thing to ask!" said
Elephant. "You know I am stronger."

"Let's find out," said Rabbit.
"Let's have a tug of war."

"Very well," said Elephant.

"Let me tie this rope to your leg,"
said Rabbit. "I will run to the middle
of our island with my end. When I give
three quick tugs, start pulling."

Rabbit ran into the woods.
He came out on the other side
of the island where Hippo lived.

"Good day, Hippo," he said.
"Which of us do you think is stronger?"

"I am," said Hippo with a laugh.

"Let's find out," said Rabbit.
"Let's have a tug of war."

Rabbit tied the end of the rope
around Hippo's leg. "Don't pull until
I give three quick tugs," he said.

Then he ran back to the middle of the island. Elephant and Hippo could not see him in the trees.

He gave three quick tugs on the middle of the rope.

From his side of the island, Elephant pulled. He tugged with all his might.

On the other side of the island, Hippo tugged back. He was right by the water. He pulled as hard as he could.

So did Elephant. He was at the edge of the water.

Both of them pulled and tugged.
But they could not move each other.

Rabbit watched them and laughed. "Now for the best part of my trick," he said. Quickly, he cut through the middle of the rope.

There were two big splashes!
And that was the end of the tug of war.

Rabbit laughed and laughed.
But he went out of his way not to see Elephant and Hippo for a few days.

UNIT TWO

Here and There,
Then and Now

King Midas and the Golden Touch

by

NATHANIEL HAWTHORNE

There was once a king named Midas. King Midas loved gold. He kept his bags of gold in a locked room.

Some days Midas would just stay in that room, counting his gold.

He had a daughter named Marygold. His love for her was great.

"My child," he would say to her. "I wish I could give you all the gold in the world. I wish that everything I touched would turn to gold."

Then Marygold would laugh.
She loved her father dearly. But she
did not care about gold.

One day as Midas counted his money,
a shadow fell upon his piles of gold.

He looked up. A man dressed in gold
was there with him!

Midas knew he had locked the door.
How had this man come in? He must
have great powers.

"You are rich, Midas," the man said.
"No other room on earth holds
as much gold as this room of yours."

"I have done well," said King Midas.
"But I would like to have still more gold."

"I heard a wish that you made,"
said the man. "You told Marygold
you wished everything you touched
would turn into gold."

"That is true," said Midas.

61

"My powers are great," said the man.
"I can make your wish come true.
Are you sure that the golden touch
would make you happy?"

"Oh, yes," said King Midas. "I am
quite sure."

The man waved his hand. "You now
have THE GOLDEN TOUCH," he said.
And he was gone.

At once the king's clothes turned
to gold. Then he touched his table.
It turned to gold.

He hurried outside and touched
the ivy on his walls. Each green leaf
became a golden leaf.

A fly landed on his nose.
But it fell to the ground at once.
It, too, had turned into gold.

He came in to touch the dishes.
First he turned Marygold's dish
to gold.

"This will be a good surprise
for my child," said Midas.

While he waited for Marygold, he thought he would read a book.

But when he touched the book, it turned to gold.

"Well," he said. "I'm hungry." He picked up a hot cake to eat. But it, too, turned to gold.

He frowned. "I don't quite see how I am going to get any lunch."

He picked up his glass.

At once his milk turned to gold. It was hard and heavy and yellow. He could not drink it.

"I don't know what is to become of me," cried Midas.

He put his head down in his hands. He was hungry now. He did not want to think how hungry he would be at bedtime.

Just then Marygold ran in and gave him a hug.

"My dear child," he said.

But she could not answer. For Marygold was no longer a child. She was a golden statue.

King Midas cried out, "Marygold!"

67

And all at once the man dressed in gold was again with him.

"I gave you your wish," he said to the king. "Has the golden touch made you happy?"

"No!" cried Midas. "I have lost my dear daughter, Marygold. If only I could have her back!"

"Maybe I can help you," the man said. "Do you really want to be done with the golden touch?"

"Oh, yes," said the king. "Gold means nothing to me now."

"You are wiser than you were, Midas," said the man.

"Help me," said the king. "I'd give all my gold to have my child again."

"Then pour water from the stream on all the things you wish to change back from gold," said the man.

King Midas ran to the stream.

He hurried to pour the water
on the gold statue of his daughter.

As soon as the water touched her,
she changed back into Marygold.

"Stop, Father," she cried. "You have
wet my nice dress." She did not know
that she had been a golden statue.

And King Midas never told her.
But he never forgot that she was dearer
to him than all the gold in the world.

Peanuts and King Midas

by

CHARLES M. SCHULZ

Reprinted by permission of UFS, Inc.

71

Early to Bed and Early to Rise

by

BENJAMIN FRANKLIN

Early to bed and early to rise

Makes a man healthy, wealthy, and wise.

72

I Started Early

by

EMILY DICKINSON

I started early, took my dog,

And visited the sea.

The mermaids in the basement

Came out to look at me.

73

The Fox and the Grapes

from
AESOP'S FABLES

There was once a hungry fox. He saw some grapes. But they were hanging over a high fence.

They looked so good!

He jumped for the lowest bunch of grapes.

But he could not reach them. He jumped again, and missed again.

74

Then he took a running start
and jumped as high as he could.
But the grapes were still out of reach.

He kept trying until he was tired out.
At last he turned away, still hungry.

"Those grapes are not worth
one more jump," said the fox.
"I did not want them anyway.
I am sure they are sour grapes."

**Sometimes we pretend
that what we cannot get
is not worth having.**

The First Tooth

by

CHARLES AND MARY LAMB

Through the house what busy joy,
Just because the infant boy
Has a tiny tooth to show!
I have got a double row.

Pease Porridge Hot

from

MOTHER GOOSE

Pease porridge hot,

pease: slap your knees
porridge: clap your hands
hot: clap partner's hands

Pease porridge cold,

same actions

Pease porridge in the pot

pease: slap your knees
porridge: clap your hands
in the: clap right hand with partner's
pot: clap your hands

Nine days old.

nine: clap left hand with partner's
days: clap your hands
old: clap partner's hands

Some like it hot.

same actions as first verse

Some like it cold.

Some like it in the pot

Nine days old.

This Little Pig Went to Market
from
MOTHER GOOSE

This little pig went to market.
big toe

This little pig stayed home.
second toe

This little pig had roast beef.
middle toe

This little pig had none.
fourth toe

And this little pig cried,
"Wee, wee, wee,"
All the way home.
little toe

The Little Turtle

by

VACHEL LINDSAY

There was a little turtle.

He lived in a box.

He swam in a puddle.

He climbed on the rocks.

He snapped at a mosquito.

He snapped at a flea.

He snapped at a minnow.

And he snapped at me.

He caught the mosquito.

He caught the flea.

He caught the minnow.

But he didn't catch me.

The Tortoise and the Hare

from
AESOP'S FABLES

Once there was a hare
who could run very fast.

Most of the other animals
did not want to race with him.
They knew he could beat them.

"Will you race with me?"
the hare asked the rat.

"No," said the rat.
"You are too fast for me."

Then the hare saw a tortoise.
He wanted to have some fun.

"Hello, my friend," he said.
"Do come and race with me."

"Very well," said the tortoise.
"But I will beat you. I will win
the race."

The rabbit laughed. "You?
But you are so slow."

"We will see," said the tortoise.
"I may be slow, but I keep going."

So they lined up to start.
And away they went.

The hare ran fast. Soon he was far ahead. So he sat down to rest.

When the tortoise caught up, the hare was fast asleep.

On went the tortoise. He said, "I won't take a rest even if I am tired. I'll keep going."

At last, when the hare woke up, it was too late.

There was the tortoise, right at the finish line. And he was laughing.

The one who keeps going can win the race.

83

An Alphabet

by

EDWARD LEAR

A

A was once an apple pie,

Pidy

Widy

Tidy

Pidy

Nice insidy

Apple Pie!

B

B was once a little bear,

Beary

Wary

Hairy

Beary

Taky cary,

Little Bear!

C

C was once a little cake,

Caky

Baky

Maky

Caky

Taky caky,

Little Cake!

Fuzzy Wuzzy

Fuzzy Wuzzy was a bear.
Fuzzy Wuzzy had no hair.
So Fuzzy Wuzzy wasn't fuzzy.
Was he?

UNIT THREE

The Whole Story

Ask Mr. Bear

story and pictures by
MARJORIE FLACK

Once there was a boy named Danny.
One day Danny's mother had a birthday.
Danny said to himself,

"What shall I give

my mother

for her

birthday?"

So Danny started out to see what he could find.
He walked along, and he met a Hen.
"Good morning, Mrs. Hen,"
said Danny.
"Can you give me
something for
my mother's
birthday?"

"Cluck, cluck," said the Hen. "I can give you
a nice fresh egg for your mother's birthday."
"Thank you," said Danny. "But she has an egg."
"Let's see
        what we
                can find then,"
                        said the Hen.

So Danny and the Hen

skipped along  until they met a Goose.

"Good morning, Mrs. Goose," said Danny.

"Can you give me
something for
my mother's
birthday?"

"Honk, honk," said the Goose. "I can give you
   some nice feathers to make a fine pillow
   for your mother's birthday."
"Thank you," said Danny. "But she has a pillow."
"Let's see
             what we
                      can find then,"
                                  said the Goose.

So Danny

and the Hen

and the Goose

all hopped along until they met

a Goat.

"Good morning, Mrs. Goat," said Danny.

"Can you give me
something
for my mother's
birthday?"

"Maa, maa," said the Goat. "I can give you
  milk for making cheese."
"Thank you," said Danny. "But she has
  some cheese."
"Let's see
          what we can find then,"
                          said the Goat.

So Danny and the Hen and the Goose

and the Goat all galloped along until they met

a Sheep.

"Good morning, Mrs. Sheep," said Danny.

"Can you give me something

for my mother's birthday?"

"Baa, baa," said the Sheep. "I can give you some wool to make a warm blanket for your mother's birthday."

"Thank you," said Danny. "But she has a blanket."

"Let's see what we can find then," said the Sheep.

So Danny and the Hen and the Goose

106

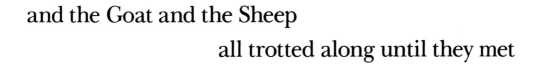

and the Goat and the Sheep

all trotted along until they met

a Cow.

"Good morning, Mrs. Cow," said Danny.
"Can you give me something for my
mother's birthday?"

"Moo, moo," said the Cow. "I can give you some
milk and cream."

"Thank you," said Danny. "But she has some
milk and cream."

"Then ask Mr. Bear," said the Cow.

"He lives in the woods over the hill."

"All right," said Danny. "Let's go and ask
Mr. Bear."

"No," said the Hen.

"No," said the Goose.

"No," said the Goat.

"No," said the Sheep.

"No—no," said the Cow.

So Danny went alone to find Mr. Bear.

He ran and he ran until he came to a hill. And

he walked and he walked

until he came to the woods. And

there he met—

115

Mr. Bear.

"Good morning, Mr. Bear," said Danny. "Can you give me something for my mother's birthday?"

"Hum, hum," said the Bear. "I have nothing to give you for your mother's birthday. But I can tell you something you can give her."

So Mr. Bear
whispered a secret
in Danny's ear.
"Oh," said Danny.
"Thank you,
Mr. Bear."

Then he ran through the woods and he skipped down the hill. And he came to his house.

"Guess what I have for your birthday!"

Danny said to his mother.

So his mother tried to guess.

"Is it an egg?"
"No, it isn't an egg," said Danny.

"Is it a pillow?"
"No, it isn't a pillow," said Danny.

"Is it a cheese?"
"No, it isn't a cheese," said Danny.

"Is it a blanket?"
"No, it isn't a blanket," said Danny.

"Is it milk or cream?"
"No, it isn't milk or cream," said Danny.

His mother could not guess at all. So—

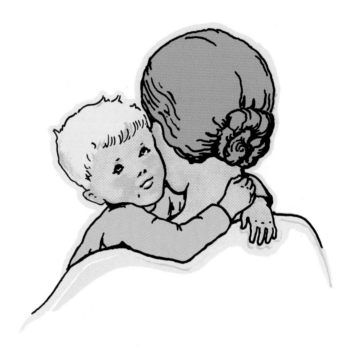

Danny gave his mother
 a Big Birthday
  Bear Hug.

UNIT FOUR

Numbers, Nature, and Nonsense

One, Two, Buckle My Shoe

from

MOTHER GOOSE

One, two,
Buckle my shoe.

Three, four,
Shut the door.

Five, six,
Pick up sticks.

Seven, eight,
Lay them straight.

Nine, ten,

A big fat hen.

Baa, Baa, Black Sheep

from

MOTHER GOOSE

Baa, baa, black sheep,
Have you any wool?
Yes, sir, yes, sir,
Three bags full.

One for my master
And one for my dame
And one for the little boy
Who lives down the lane.

129

Three Blind Mice

from

MOTHER GOOSE

Three blind mice. Three blind mice.

See how they run. See how they run.

They all ran after the farmer's wife

Who cut off their tails with a carving knife,

Did you ever see such a sight in your life,

As three blind mice?

Sing a Song of Six Pence

from

MOTHER GOOSE

Sing a song of six pence
Pocket full of rye.
Five and twenty blackbirds
Baked in a pie.

When the pie was opened,
The birds began to sing.
Now wasn't that a dainty dish
To set before a king!

The Three Little Pigs and the Big Bad Wolf

A PLAY

adapted from an English folktale

Speaking Parts
Narrator
First Pig
Second Pig
Third Pig
Big Bad Wolf

Narrator   Once upon a time there were three little pigs. The first little pig built a house of straw. The Big Bad Wolf came to his door and knocked.

Wolf   Little pig, little pig, let me come in.

First Pig   No, no, not by the hair of my chinny chin chin.

Wolf   Then I'll huff and I'll puff and I'll blow your house in.

Narrator And the Big Bad Wolf did
huff and puff. And he did blow down
the house of straw.

135

Wolf Now I'll eat you up.

First Pig (running) You must catch me first. I'm off to the house of my brother.

Narrator His brother was the second little pig. That little pig had built a house of sticks.
  The Big Bad Wolf chased the first little pig down the hill. That little pig ran into the house of his brother and locked the door. The wolf knocked.

Wolf Little pig, little pig, let me come in.

Second Pig No, no, not by the hair of my chinny chin chin.

Wolf Then I'll huff and I'll puff and I'll blow your house in.

Narrator The wolf did huff and puff. He did blow down the house of sticks.

Wolf   Now I will eat both of you.
   What a fine dinner!

First and Second Pigs (running)   You
   must catch us first. We are off
   to the house of our brother.

137

Narrator   Their brother was the third little pig. He had built a house of bricks.

The Big Bad Wolf chased the pigs across the field. They ran inside their brother's brick house and locked the door. The wolf knocked.

Wolf   Little pig, little pig, let me come in.

Third Pig   No, no, not by the hair of my chinny chin chin.

Wolf   Then I'll huff and I'll puff and I'll blow your house in.

Narrator   The wolf huffed and puffed. He puffed and huffed. But he could not blow down the house of bricks.

Wolf   I've huffed and I've puffed 'til my face has turned blue. But you can't get away. Little pigs, I'll get you.

Narrator   The Big Bad Wolf climbed up
on the third pig's roof and started
down the chimney.

139

Wolf   Little pigs, little pigs, I am not through. I'm coming in. And I'll get you.

Third Pig   My brothers and I have a surprise for you.

Narrator   The three pigs put a big pot of water on the fire. In fell the wolf as he came down the chimney.

Third Pig   Now we will eat you up.

Narrator   And that is just what the three pigs did. They cooked the wolf, ate him for dinner, and lived happily ever after.

If a Pig Wore a Wig

by

CHRISTINA ROSSETTI

If a pig wore a wig,
What could we say?
Treat him as a gentleman
And say, "Good day."

The Crow and the Pitcher

from

ASEOP'S FABLES

There was once a crow who was very thirsty.

He flew down to a farmer's yard. There on the ground he saw a pitcher. It had a little water in it.

The crow tried to get a drink. But he could not reach the water. It was too far down in the pitcher.

"I will find a way to get that water," said the crow.

As he walked around the pitcher, he saw a stone on the ground.

It gave him an idea.

He dropped that stone in the pitcher. Then another stone. And still another.

Each time a stone fell into the pitcher, the water rose a little.

At last the water was high enough for the crow to get his drink.

Little by little does the trick.

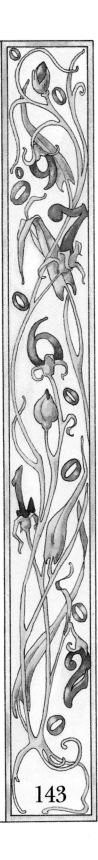

143

Humpty Dumpty

from

MOTHER GOOSE

Humpty Dumpty sat on a wall.
Humpty Dumpty had a great fall.
All the king's horses and all the king's men
Couldn't put Humpty together again.

Humpty Dumpty and Alice

from

THROUGH THE LOOKING-GLASS

by

LEWIS CARROLL

Alice took a good look at Humpty Dumpty. He really was shaped like an egg. But he was very well dressed.

"What a nice belt," said Alice.

"Yes," said Humpty Dumpty. "It is a fine belt. The King and Queen gave it to me. It's an un-birthday present."

Alice looked puzzled. "What is an un-birthday present?"

"A present given when it is not your birthday, of course," said Humpty.

Alice thought about that. "I like birthday presents best," she said at last.

"You do not know what you are talking about!" cried Humpty. "How many days are there in a year?"

"Three hundred and sixty-five," said Alice.

"Right," said Humpty. "And how many birthdays have you?"

"One," said Alice.

"And if you take one from three hundred and sixty-five, what is left?" asked Humpty.

"Three hundred and sixty-four, of course," Alice said quickly.

"Wait," said Humpty. "That may not be right. I want to see that done on paper."

Alice could not help smiling as she took out a paper. She wrote the numbers for him.

$$365$$
$$\underline{-1}$$
$$364$$

Humpty took the paper. He looked at it. "Well," he began. "That seems to be right—"

"You are holding it upside down," said Alice.

"So I was," Humpty said.

She turned it around for him.

"That is better," said Humpty. "It looked a little strange before. But now it shows that I am right."

"What?" said Alice.

"Don't you see?" said Humpty. "There are three hundred and sixty-four days when you might get un-birthday presents."

"Yes," Alice said slowly.

"And only one day for birthday presents," Humpty went on. "That is why I like un-birthday presents better."

Bubbles

by

CARL SANDBURG

Two bubbles found they had rainbows
  on their curves.

They flickered out saying:

"It was worth being a bubble just to have held
  that rainbow thirty seconds."

The Elves and the Shoemaker

by the

BROTHERS GRIMM

There was once an old shoemaker who was very poor.

One night he said to his wife, "I have leather to make one last pair of shoes. We must sell them. Or we will have no money for food."

He cut out the shoes that night to work on the next day.

But in the morning he found the pair of shoes finished.

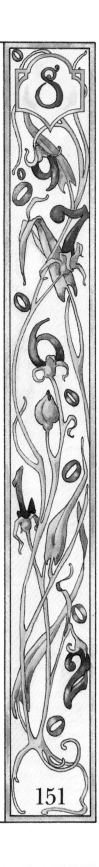

151

"How can this be?" the old man thought. He looked at each shoe.

Every stitch was right. They were the finest shoes he ever saw.

Soon a man came in to buy shoes. He tried on the new pair. The shoes fit him very well.

So he was willing to pay a good bit of money for them.

Now the shoemaker could buy leather for two more pairs of shoes. He cut them out that night. And he meant to work on them the next day.

But he did not need to. When he got up, they were finished.

That day he sold the two pairs of shoes. Then he had money to buy leather for four pairs of shoes.

He cut them out that night. Then he went to bed.

In the morning the old man found four fine pairs of shoes on his table.

And so it went on and on.

Soon he was rich.

One night he said to his wife, "Let us sit up and see who comes here."

So they left a candle burning.
Then they hid in a corner of the room
behind some coats. And they watched.

Late at night, in came two little elves.
They sat down at the shoemaker's table.
The little elves began to stitch the shoes
with their tiny fingers.

They did not stop until all the shoes
were finished.

Then they ran away.

The next day the shoemaker's wife was up early. "Those elves looked cold last night," she said to him. "I will make coats for them. And you should make two tiny pairs of shoes."

"Yes," he said. "That is just what we should do." He got right to work.

That night their presents were ready. They put the clothes on the table. Two coats and two tiny pairs of shoes! Then they hid in the corner again.

The elves came in, ready to work.
They looked around for the leather.
Then they saw the tiny coats and shoes!

The elves put on their new clothes
and started to sing.

"Now we're dressed so fine and neat.
  Why make shoes for other's feet?"

How they danced and hopped about!
How they shouted for joy! And at last
they danced out the door.

The elves were never seen again.
But all went well for the shoemaker
and his wife as long as they lived.

A·C·K·N·O·W·L·E·D·G·M·E·N·T·S

Acknowledgment is gratefully made to the following individuals and publishers for permission to reprint these selections.

"I Started Early." Reprinted from *The Complete Poems of Emily Dickinson*, edited by Thomas H. Johnson, published by Little, Brown and Company.

"The Little Turtle." Reprinted with permission of Macmillan Publishing Company from *Collected Poems* by Vachel Lindsay. © 1920 by Macmillan Publishing Company, renewed 1948 by Elizabeth C. Lindsay.

Ask Mr. Bear. Reprinted with permission of Macmillan Publishing Company from *Ask Mr. Bear* by Marjorie Flack. © 1932 by Macmillan Publishing Company, renewed 1960 by Hilma H. Barnum.

"Bubbles." From *The Complete Poems of Carl Sandburg,* Revised and Expanded Edition, © 1950 by Carl Sandburg and renewed 1978 by Margaret Sandburg, Helga Sandburg Crile, and Janet Sandburg, reprinted with permission of Harcourt Brace Jovanovich, Inc.

The following poems are excerpted from longer poems in consideration of the ages of the readers:

"Block City" by Robert Louis Stevenson

"I Started Early" by Emily Dickinson

"The First Tooth" by Charles and Mary Lamb

"If a Pig Wore a Wig" by Christina Rossetti

157

I·L·L·U·S·T·R·A·T·I·O·N C·R·E·D·I·T·S

Acknowledgment is gratefully made to the following for permission to reprint these illustrations.

PAGE	ILLUSTRATOR
8–9	Kate Greenaway. Reprinted by permission of The Huntington Library, San Marino, California.
10–11	Berta and Elmer Hader. © 1987 by Derrydale Books, a division of Crown Publishers, Inc.
13	Arthur Rackham. The Central Children's Room, Donnell Library Center, The New York Public Library.
15	Unknown.
17	Jennie Harbour.
19	Arthur Rackham. Reprinted by permission of The Huntington Library, San Marino, California.
21	C. L. Fraser.
22–33	L. Leslie Brooke. Edith Wetmore Collection of Children's Books, Providence Public Library.
35, 39	Pamela R. Levy. © 1991 by Jamestown Publishers, Inc. All rights reserved.
36, 42	Arthur Rackham.
41	Edmund Dulac. General Research Division. The New York Public Library. Astor, Lenox, and Tilden Foundations.
45	Milo Winter. From *The Aesop for Children*, illustrated by Milo Winter. © 1919, 1947 by Checkerboard Press, a division of Macmillan, Inc. All rights reserved.

47, 48	Pamela R. Levy. © 1991 by Jamestown Publishers, Inc. All rights reserved.
49	Jessie Willcox Smith.
50–55	Jerry Pinkney. © 1991 by Jamestown Publishers, Inc. All rights reserved.
61, 63, 69	Pamela R. Levy. © 1991 by Jamestown Publishers, Inc. All rights reserved.
59, 65, 67	Arthur Rackham. The Central Children's Room, Donnell Library Center, The New York Public Library.
72	Berta and Elmer Hader. © 1987 by Derrydale Books, a division of Crown Publishers, Inc.
73	Bob Eggleton. © 1991 by Jamestown Publishers, Inc. All rights reserved.
74–75	Arthur Rackham.
76	Tom Feelings. From *Something On My Mind,* words by Nikki Grimes, pictures by Tom Feelings. Pictures © 1978 by Tom Feelings. Reproduced by permission of the publisher, Dial Books for Young Readers.
77	Thomas Ewing Malloy. © 1991 by Jamestown Publishers, Inc. All rights reserved.
78	Jessie Willcox Smith.
79	Bob Eggleton. © 1991 by Jamestown Publishers, Inc. All rights reserved.
81	Arthur Rackham. Reprinted by permission of The Huntington Library, San Marino, California.
82, 83	Pamela R. Levy. © 1991 by Jamestown Publishers, Inc. All rights reserved.
84–86	Edward Lear.

160